I See You... Wonderful You!

Your Disability is your ABILITY

By: Tanya Salmon

This is a work of creative nonfiction. Some parts have been fictionalized in varying degrees, for various purposes.

Copyright © 2023 by Tanya Salmon

All rights reserved. No part of this book may be reproduced or used in any manner without written permission of the copyright owner except for the use of quotations in a book review. For more information, contact: awriterscraft@gmail.com.

First Edition
First Hardcover and eBook edition: August 2023

Book design and illustrations by bobooks

ISBN 978-1-7390008-0-6 (Hardcover)
ISBN 978-1-7390008-1-3 (ebook)

www.awriterscraft.ca

For my Clara.
In knowing all the things that you CAN do.

All children are capable of great things.

I see you constantly making your own sense of the world with a bold curiosity.

I see you as able; doing the same things your friends can do, *just in your own way in your own time.*

uncovering your God-given gifts.

www.ingramcontent.com/pod-product-compliance
Lightning Source LLC
Chambersburg PA
CBHW082041200426
43209CB00053B/1335